Crooked Trees: Buil

Printed in the United States of America

First Printing, 2019

ISBN 9781095035047

To: Kelly,
Thank you so much
for your support.
Love
E Vasser

Crooked Trees

Building on A Fragile Foundation

By Eboni L. Vasser

Acknowledgments

The challenge of making acknowledgments is name-calling because there will always be someone who has played a pivotal part of your journey that you will forget to mention. With a book of this nature, you have a lot of silent contributors, who without their stories, you would have nothing to talk about when writing a book. With that being said, I am limiting including names. I would like to first start off with my husband. As soon as I really settled down and told him how much I wanted to write a book, he purchased me a computer as a gift. He attempted to hide it but was unsuccessful.

I want to thank my daughter Antania because she has always had faith in me, even during the challenging times when I was a single mother and struggled to keep the utilities on. While working long hours, she never complained nor put me in a position to ever have to come to her school for any disciplinary problems. She always made the joy of raising a child alone much easier because she took instruction with integrity and did what was right.

I want to thank my family in its entirety, whether it be my parents, brothers, aunts and uncles, cousins or whomever- at some point in my life, they all reprimanded me about procrastinating when it came to writing my book.

I want to thank every member of Abba's Heart Inc. who has invested their time in making sure the purpose of God for my life is fulfilled completely.

I want to thank my Pastors, Apostle and Mrs. Victor L. Hill, for their patience in my journey of overcoming generational wounds and their spiritual fortitude in assuring me that God will make sure deliverance takes place in my life.

Crooked Trees: Building on a Fragile Foundation

Lastly, I want to thank the members of Providence Christian Ministries for being a ministry that is focused on " Building Healthy Families for the Kingdom".

I have several friends who are also a part of this journey who, just like my family, refused to let me get away with not writing. I limited name calling only because there is an entire village behind the writing of this book and there is no way I would ever be able to address the countless people who played a part. I thank each of you from the bottom of my heart.

I want to thank my book coach, Charrisa T. Without her, I may have been stuck on step two of a five step journey. She made sure this book was completed with ease. I recommend her to anyone who wants to write a book.

Table of Contents

Introduction

Families everywhere have adopted the symbol of the tree as a way of showing its foundation. Through the branches on the tree, families can link the patriarch and matriarch of the family to those who have gone ahead of them and those who have come after them. Though the tree links the actual ancestry, the tree fails to tell the entire story. The tree does not tell the details of dysfunction, such as, hereditary illnesses or generational dysfunctions. It tells us our ancestors' name but fails to tell us the bad habits that we acquire as a result of bad behaviors that existed before us.

Most of us come from the era where we were told, "What happens in this house, stays in this house." We gained more from our family than just a name. We were not taught to get help for our shortcomings, but we were taught to act as if our shortcomings did not exist. Because of how we were raised, we tend to not seek assistance for the fragile foundations that have molded the way we react to the stressors of life. We fail to recognize generational behavior and decisions that our parents and even their parents made that affect us in our present-day decisions. There are men struggling with infidelity and lust that are unaware of the struggles of the men in the family that came before them. There are women who have multiple children out of wedlock that fail to realize that there are other women within the family that had the same struggle. There are people within a family with mental illness that are afraid to get help because they are unaware that they have other family members who suffered from mental illness.

Our inability to share family secrets have literally disabled others within the bloodline from getting a proper understanding of where the origin of their struggle began. Just as strengths are inherited, so are weaknesses. Once we get a better understanding of our weaknesses, the better able we are at resolving our issues

Crooked Trees: Building on a Fragile Foundation

while breaking the chain of dysfunction from our bloodlines. There was much research that went into writing this book. A lot of it was professional in the form of research from a psychological perspective and others were just personal documentaries that confirm that bad behavior resulted from childhood events that took place while in the care of our parents, grandparents, and so forth. We hear stories of substance abuse that flow down from generation to generation. We see lifestyle similarities whether good or bad, in the lives of grandparents, parents, aunts, uncles, siblings, cousins and other distant relatives.

We have no problem giving our primary care physician details about our medical history, but we fail to take in account the effects of our generational history. We are not ashamed to say both grandparents had high blood pressure and that it runs in our family history, but fail to speak on molestation from fathers, uncles, and even brothers. We do not mind sharing that our mother or grandmother had diabetes, but we do not speak on how divorce could run prevalent in the lives of the women of our family. In a brief conversation once with some of my paternal cousins, we found that several of us suffered from fibroids and endometriosis. During that conversation, I was able to inform them of my own battle with fibroids while another close family member suffered from endometriosis. We will share the fact that breast cancer has affected both my maternal and paternal side, but no one speaks of substance abuse or alcoholism. No one shares about abuse.

Once, I had a cousin to tell of a story about my paternal grandfather abusing my dad and his siblings. I stood in amazement at the fact that I was an adult and never knew that my dad was physically, verbally, and emotionally abused. For the longest, because I was younger, I believed that my grandfather only abused my grandmother. What I heard next absolutely turned my stomach! I asked my dad about him being abused as a child and he said because he had forgiven my grandfather when he gave his life to Christ, he felt like he should not talk about it and defame his character. Still, when I found myself in a relationship with an abusive man, everyone seemed to be amazed that I would accept such foolery in my life. Later I found that my maternal grandfather, whom I had a perfect relationship with, was also a participant of domestic violence. I would hear stories of how both, my maternal and paternal grandmothers, suffered abuse at the hands of my grandfathers. Somehow, I could not help but to wonder, if this type of abuse subconsciously found its way to me. No one in either side linked my acceptance of abuse to either situation. It was as if my situation was isolated and I lived in an era where I should have known better.

Thing is, my abuser, also witnessed the abuse of his mother from his step-father and I also witnessed his mom referring to his sisters with derogatory phrases when speaking to them. There are so many dysfunctions that are birthed in families and until someone begins to educate themselves in recovery, the family will continue to suffer. No one had a problem referring to my mom's athleticism when I was the star basketball player in high school and college. They would always brag on my mom's ability to play basketball and run track. Whenever I balanced my checkbook to the penny, everyone would always say how well my maternal grandfather could budget his finances. How many people are taught the good without anyone addressing the bad and the ugly? How many of us are left with a thorn in our side without anyone else accepting the part they played in our dysfunction?

I do not have to make up examples in order to prove a point in this book. I have enough personal stories from family members or friends to fill the pages of this book. This subject is so prevalent that even upon completion of this book, there is so much that had to be left out for sake of time and space. When friends tell you that their step-fathers have molested them and they never told. It was a secret they allowed their step-father to take to the grave. Their mothers never knowing their innocence was taken by a man she laid beside every night. When you have family members that were violated time and time again by friends of the family and to your knowledge no arrests were ever made, and no counseling ever sought. Lives destroyed decades later because no one properly handled emotional recovery. We were just taught to be strong and pray our way through. Still, once those connected to us give their lives to Christ, they believe prayer can deliver us from wounds that are so deep that it magnifies our dysfunction.

I am delivered personally from the impact of my past. However, it was not through faith alone that I became delivered. At the time my deliverance came, it was a combination effort of professional counseling, pastoral counseling, exercising, faith confessions, prayer, and being sick and tired of being tired. I began a journey of realizing that my dysfunction was bigger than me. I was not the sole perpetrator in my emotional demise. There were a lot of contributors and whether they accepted ownership in the part they played or not, I would no longer accept anyone calling me crazy or mentally unstable. I would no longer accept people acting like they did not know what was wrong with me. Even in my realizing that there were more culprits than admittance, I also realized that those who played a part in my pain also needed guidance in how to be delivered from their own pain. Instead of me holding a grudge, I begin to feel sorry for us all.

I have never been molested as a child but endured sexual abuse from the hands of my abuser as an adult. At first, I did not realize it was rape because he was my boyfriend. It was only after watching television that I realized that it was date rape. No meant no even if it was your boyfriend. It was only after I escaped that I begin to see the driving force behind his anger. Just as I was let down because of my family dynamics, so was he. Just as my parents were let down because of their family dynamics, so were my grandparents, and so on. Time and time again, families leave an inheritance for their children, and the things we inherit are not always blessings, but curses. It is unfair to label someone crazy and off-balance when you know they have suffered abuse, neglect, and other dysfunctions early in their lives. It is so unfair to speak of violent crime without addressing the fact that abusers were once victims of crime.

We do not even relate racism as dysfunction. Even though we know it had to be taught by generations before that taught others how to hate. Dysfunction has destroyed so many families and until we make the choice to stop it, it will continue to destroy our lives. There was once a time when dysfunction only destroyed a household, but now dysfunction destroys a community. When you have wounded children going into schools and killing other children, that is a problem that needs to be stopped. When you have women being trafficked for sex, that is a problem that needs to be addressed. When you have people, who are not afraid of the consequences of killing others, robbing others, raping others, etc. These are problems that need to be addressed. We do not have a mental illness problem, nor do we have a substance abuse problem. We do not have a crime problem, we have a dysfunction problem. What we see today is a world filled with a lot of isolated family issues that were not properly addressed. There are some legitimate mental illnesses in this world, but not everything we are addressing as a mental illness is one of those.

Dysfunction has destroyed so many families and until we make the choice to stop it, it will continue to destroy our lives.

Why a Tree?

Accding to Wikipedia, using the image of the tree to represent family probably originated in the medieval art of the Tree of Jesse, used to illustrate the Genealogy of Christ in accordance with Isaiah 11:1. *And there shall come forth a rod out of the stem of Jesse, and a branch shall grow out of his roots.* The use of the tree in symbolism other than spiritual schemes involves the trees of classical gods in Boccaccio's Genealogia deorum gentilium. The family tree is so prevalent today that there are websites and apps that assist people in building their family tree. If you were to research the phrase family tree, the definition given is genealogy. Synonyms given are ancestry, birth, blood, bloodline, breeding, descent, extraction, line, lineage, origin, parentage, pedigree, stick, and strain. The first known use of the family tree was in 1763 as mentioned by Merriam-Webster dictionary.

My first recollection of the family tree was a family reunion t-shirt worn as a child. Symbolic of the dysfunction presented, I only recall the matriarch of the family being displayed on the shirt. The patriarch of the family was never added to the shirt. At that time, my family did not realize that subtracting the patriarch from the family was dysfunctional in itself. My great-grandmother, Elnora Singleton, could not make children alone and even if there was something distasteful in their marriage, there was a need to know what happened. Though a reunion is a time to celebrate family, this is one of the few times when a large quantity of family members come together. Therefore, history of the family should be given in totality while making mention of where the family name comes from.

I am not insinuating that dirty laundry should be made public at a family reunion celebration. I am just saying no name should be left behind. That way, when we return home from our celebration, it can promote healthy discussions about our entire

Crooked Trees: Building on a Fragile Foundation

family history. I also noticed on the shirts that my grandfather was listed as the only son of my great grandmother, but I later found out he had a brother. They did not keep in contact with him and I cannot share the story of why he left because I never knew a valid reason only rumors. I do not know if my great-grandfather was a man of integrity. All I know is that my great-grandmother was left to raise her children and did anything she could, including shoplifting, to take care of her children. Keep in mind, I am not sharing this information to shed any negative light on my family. There were a lot of prominent people in my family who did things the legal way, I am only contributing to the future content of this book.

Before I get ahead of myself, I want to return to the aspect of the tree. In school, I learned a lot about a tree. I remember knowing that if you saw a tree trunk where a tree had been cut, that the circles within the trunk can tell you how old the tree was. I know the roots of the tree could go various lengths underground depending on how old it was. The older it was, the stronger those roots which made it impossible for a tree to be uprooted unless it was broken at the trunk. Trees can be several thousand years old and have been in existence for 370 million years. The trunk contains woody tissue for strength and vascular tissue to carry materials from one part of the tree to another. The ancient Greeks developed a classification about 300 B.C.E. in which plants were grouped according to their general form-that is, as trees, shrubs, undershrub, and vines. This classification was used for almost 1000 years. Research in both Wikipedia and Britannica show that the root of trees provide the foundation (anchorage) and absorption of enough water and nutrients to support the remainder of the tree.

I once heard a preacher preach a sermon using a palm tree as an illustration. I do not recall her name to reference her statement, but she caught my attention while referring to a palm tree being a tree that will bend but won't break. This caused me to research the palm tree out of curiosity. A palm tree is a monocot and maples and oaks are dicots. Therefore, a palm tree can endure the winds in a storm, and they will bend and not break. According

Crooked Trees: Building on a Fragile Foundation

to www.livescience.com, trees generally snap, or at least lose a few branches, when faced with hurricane-strength wind. Not palm trees. These staples of the tropics typically bend during gusty weather. In the same article, Laura Geggel, states that palm trees are not made of wood like other trees. They are made of spongy tissue, scattered instead of arranged, inside the palm.

Where other trees have those rings I mentioned earlier, the palm tree does not have this. Why so much information about a tree? When given the right kind of water and nutrients a tree can survive for decades after decades. However, if a tree does not have enough water and nutrients, it will be difficult for it to survive. Therefore, no matter how the tree came to be the symbol of family, it shows that without a firm foundation the family will not stand. Whether the tree came about because of Isaiah 11:1 or if it came about through any other means, the fact that most of us accept it as a family symbol; we need to take into consideration what the symbol means. Like a tree, a family succeeds on the foundation by which is stands. Therefore, you hear people refer to a person's heritage when they mess up. For example, whenever Prince Harry was caught by the Paparazzi partying; the news anchors would always refer to the expected behavior of the royal family. When you have a President in office, there is a certain level of expectation concerning the behavior of the members of their family. Depending on the foundation that has been laid out concerning your surname, there is an expectation to those who bear that name.

We do not have to be famous for our surname to matter. Being known in your community alone can link you to this level of expectation. You can watch the news and if a mother is well known and respected in her community, if her son is caught doing something that does not represent her well, people will comment. You have heard people say, "That is Agnes' boy." "We wouldn't have ever expected this kind of behavior out of him." In times past, it is believed that we took pride in building strong foundations for our families. I believe this is how family secrets got started. It is as if we act one way in the limelight and less appealing behavior is

Crooked Trees: Building on a Fragile Foundation

done in the dark. For this reason, we hear songs like, "Papa was a rolling stone-wherever he laid his hat was his home." Therefore, we show up at a funeral and there are a multitude of children there mourning a father while having mothers other than his wife. Because we do not discuss the shaky roots of the family tree, we find generations later that a great-great and sometimes a great, great, great grandson will suffer from the same infidelities of the great, great, great grandfather that came before him.

The foundation of a family is just as important as the root of the tree. The origin of that tree determines the strength of the tree. The foundation determines the longevity and whether the other parts of the tree will be healthy. I have an uncle who has his own lawn maintenance company and he discusses the importance of pruning. My mom had a tree next to a window of her house and it was damaged in a storm. She noticed one day when she came home from work that her tree was leaning. She called my uncle and he pruned the tree, removing all the damaged branches of the tree. After he cut almost all the tree away, it looked ridiculous as if he did not know what he was doing. Before long, the tree grew back and looked healthier than ever before. If my mom would have ignored the tree, the damaged parts holding on to the healthy parts could have lessened the chances of survival. Because she contacted my uncle and he was able to offer a method of recovery, the tree was saved.

Trees are strong and have many parts. There are times where you can see a tree after a storm and it only loses a few tiny branches. There are times when you have a storm and a tree loses nothing but a few leaves. Trees can survive through various seasons and depending on the kind of tree it is, it can bear fruit. Trees are so strong that if they fall, they can destroy anything within their path. During hot, summer days, they can also be shade from the heat of the sun. Therefore, a tree can support or destroy depending on what it is being used for at the time. A tree can be cut down and become a resource for firewood. A tree can be used for paper. A tree has several uses. How does this apply to family?

Crooked Trees: Building on a Fragile Foundation

When properly used, family can be a support. It can protect a person and support a person who is in need or it can destroy anything that is in its path. The family has many parts and when faced with trials, trees can lose a few leaves, or it can be destroyed. The family can survive many seasons. It can survive the loss of the patriarch or matriarch if the foundation is strong. It can survive a tragedy. Families can survive so much during its growth process if the foundation provided the proper nutrients for healthy growth.

Most trees are straight. They are not feeble, but bear strength. This must be a reason why the tree was chosen as the symbol of family. Still with as many attributes that the tree may offer, what happens when the tree is crooked? What happens when the foundation is not as strong as it used to be? Do we still bear the right to wear a strong symbol on our family reunion t-shirts when our family does not represent the symbol we are wearing? We counterfeit the symbol at times by acting like our family is strong knowing that behind the scenes it is weak. We take ownership of the strong tree knowing our tree shows signs of malnutrition. We do not want to talk about the things that make our foundation shaky. We continue to act like we have it altogether when we know our symbol needs work. It is not that our family is a lost cause, it's just the more we ignore the lack of nutrition, the more we cause our tree to sway. The thing is, the family tree is not a monocot like the palm. The palm tree is not the symbol that was adopted to represent family. Truth is, the family tree is a dicot and during a storm it will not bend, it will break.

We would like to believe that we can place all the pressure in the world on our symbol and it should survive. But, without roots that run deep enough to keep us standing, surviving certain storms and seasons is not possible. The foundation is not solid if the matriarch left early in the growth process of the children. The foundation is challenged if daddy was an alcoholic or gambler and left home when the children were young. The foundation is shaky when outside kids live down the street from daddy but are taught to not refer to him as daddy because he has a wife and a family.

Crooked Trees: Building on a Fragile Foundation

The tree is not strong and firm when daddy was sleeping in the bed with his daughter and later the son was sleeping in the bed with their sister. This is not the symbol of the dicot standing strong and ready to survive for thousands of years. We lose our right to use the tree as a symbol for family when we allow dysfunction to eradicate what the symbol stands for. When daddy can beat mommy behind closed doors, but when we get in the car to go grocery shopping, we act like our roots are healthy. When the eldest son feels less of a man because he cannot protect mommy not realizing his job was to be a child and not a protector. When the eldest daughter feels like it's her job to keep secret that daddy has made her his mistress. These are the things that distort the image of the family tree and instead of standing tall, it becomes crooked.

Like a tree, a family succeeds on the foundation by which is stands.

Family Dynamics

There are several different types of dysfunctional families. In this book, I choose to create definitions that come from experience rather than given by outside references.

The five effects of dysfunctional families that I have chosen are:

1. **The Chronic Conflict Effect**
2. **The Compulsive Effect**
3. **The Addictive Personality Effect**
4. **The Need for Control Effect**
5. **The Emotionally Distant Effect**

Each of the effects mentioned above are toxic, meaning, the contents of the family dynamics have contributed to the dysfunction of everyone that is connected to them. We can dress for success and look the part, but each of these categories show the reason why some of our trees are crooked.

The Chronic Conflict Effect

Growing up, this appeared to be my maternal side of the family. We could not get along for anything. Every family function we attended, there would be someone who would "show their tail." It was nothing for us to be having a great time and an altercation break out, physical and/or verbal. With the chronic conflict effect, battles continue because they are never properly resolved. Without addressing certain issues, animosity will remain, and families continue to try at being happy without discussing the pink elephant in the middle of the room. The family can never stay around each other during prolonged periods of time without someone reacting to a subject that has yet to be resolved. For years I have heard my mother and other siblings refer to another sibling as being my grandfather's favorite. Therefore, there were times that animosity showed its ugly head quite a bit.

The unresolved issues were masked and as soon as the alcohol or drug use intensified, someone responded to something said in a negative manner. It started with our parents and before long, the children joined in to this behavior. Both the medical definition and general definition of the word chronic are the same. Chronic simply means lasting a long time. It is as if anything that is chronic has no expiration date and there is a great length of difficulty in getting a solution. Still, if we had chronic asthma, we would not discontinue our medical pursuit of finding relief. If we had cancer, heart disease, or any other physical ailment; we would go to specialists no matter how long it would take and diligently journey after some sort of relief.

We accept chronic ailments when it comes to our family dynamics. We are too afraid to sit down and have a mature conversation about what is bothering us. I cannot speak for any other family, but my families' conflict was chronic because we loved to talk about things in the form of gossip without addressing the person who we were offended with. By the time the information concerning who we were mad at, made it back to the alleged offender, it had been twisted by every other family member that held the information prior to it making its way to them. Simply put, the chronic conflict effect is the family that just refuses to get along. They will not accept individual flaws, resolve painful issues, and now the family is built on a shaky foundation.

Families cannot stand firm like a tree if their entire foundation is filled with animosity. Funny thing is, individuals can get older in age, but somehow, there is still a hurt little girl or boy on the inside that needs to be healed. The cliché remains, "Hurt people, hurt people." A chronic effect is after almost sixty years of life, a person can still refer to painful events that bother them. A chronic effect is when you can put several siblings in the room, and they can all get stirred up with negative emotions if a certain topic is brought up. A chronic effect is when a parent in the family can allow their children to inherit these negative feelings, and even a child who was not present when the event happened, can still get upset because they want to defend their wounded parent.

Anything chronic has a lasting effect. No matter how much time lapses, the stench of something chronic seems impossible to make disappear. God gave me the revelation concerning the definition of a chronic effect. A chronic effect mimics this scenario. A person can be in search of a home to buy and come to the home of their dreams. The outside décor can be perfect, landscaping is immaculate, the right number of bedrooms and matching bathrooms. You get inside and there are cathedral ceilings, granite countertops, the perfect flooring, etc. Upon seeing it, you want the house immediately and the price is perfect. There is one problem, the house has a stench. It appears that a family of rodents have infiltrated the house, got into the walls and the crawlspace. They were unable to escape, and they die. Now, this home is filled with a stench that subtracts from its beauty. You cannot help but to remember it's everything you want, but after your realtor contacts the sellers, they find that they have been trying to get rid of this chronic smell for months.

Pest control companies have cleared the home of every dead rodent they can find, but there are still some remains that have not been detected. They have torn down walls and removed everything that they discovered, still there was an infestation and they have been unsuccessful in ridding the house of the stench. The price has been dropped dramatically in hopes that someone will still consider the purchase. The house has been on the market for over a year because no buyer is willing to put up with the smell. The chronic effect is this, no matter how successful you are; how much money you have; how many degrees you possess; there is something about your situation that is so unresolved that no one can get along with you. This is true for an individual or corporately for an entire family. The chronic conflict effect just shows that you are a family that has not been disciplined enough to work through any misbehavior or negative situation long enough to get it resolved. This is the family that would rather stop attending family engagements for lack of the willingness to resolve the things that are keeping them apart.

The sad truth is, this is the family that has generations coming behind them that learn to live in dysfunction and find love in negative environments for lack of family support. Children of these families run to the streets, gangs, inappropriate sexual relationships, and even traffickers because they are looking for love that they cannot get from a strong family foundation. We will uphold our truth rather than to deal with the lie that is destroying the family. We will uphold our right to be right than to submit to the possibility that we could be wrong to resolve ongoing conflict. We keep our kids from learning that family is important and as adults they enter relationships taking the baggage of what was taught with them. They never learn how to resolve conflict so without knowledge of generational history, they find themselves struggling to maintain a healthy household. This is the chronic conflict effect.

The Compulsive Effect

Compulsive means uncontrollable. It also means obsessive. What does this look like in a family? A compulsive family is like the chronic conflict family in that every reaction to a painful stimulus is not thought through. Chaos results from people not being able to carefully think through a proper response to the things that hurt them. In the compulsive effect, it is pretty much everyone feeling like they have the prerogative to do and say anything they feel like saying. It is learning to live a life with no boundaries. Everyone is stepping on everyone's toes. The compulsive effect adds fuel to the fire of chronic conflict in that, no one wants to submit to the greater good of the family. Instead of a resolution, several of the family members are out of sync and this gives them the right to always speak their mind. The compulsive effect results from wounds that run so deep along with a pride that will not allow a person to admit fault. If everyone wants to be right and everyone wants to have the final say, then nothing gets resolved.

Compulsiveness is a life without limits, and not in a good way. Compulsiveness lacks discipline and respect. A person who is compulsive speaks with no regard to how their conversation can hurt someone else. They do things with no regard to how their actions can hurt someone else. It is different from narcissism in that a person who is compulsive does not have to be arrogant, self-centered, manipulative, or demanding. Still, they are similar in that they tend to not have empathy for how their behavior comes across to those who are around them. How can this apply to a family? When you have several family members who cannot resist the urge to act in a way that is not beneficial to a loving environment, this is compulsive. It is the power to compel other members of the family to act just like you. It is the inability to refrain from language or behavior that negatively impact your family's structure or social environment.

Think in terms of a compulsive liar, this is a person who will lie about anything no matter how major or minor it may be. It is pathological behavior that becomes so normal that you no longer see anything wrong with it. Think of a compulsive eater, this is a person who overeats due to emotions or just an imbalance that triggers them to want more food. Think of the compulsive shopper, this is someone who shops even if they are in a boat load of debt. Compulsiveness in family dynamics is sudden behavior that sets no boundaries on a person's urge to act. They act before giving any thought to the consequences of their actions. They don't care how it affects another and they will defend their actions even when they can see that they have hurt someone else. When dealing with this effect in the family, people tend to walk away even more wounded than they were before. For those who are striving to become healthy, they tend to avoid family atmospheres for fear of being drawn back into dysfunction. For those who are wounded, they tend to come back to family atmospheres in hopes that something

Crooked Trees: Building on a Fragile Foundation

has changed, but often find themselves being wounded by being once again let down.

Those who have the compulsive behaviors, the antagonist of the family dysfunction, seem to instigate most of the brawls and are comfortable continuing in the dysfunctional behavior. Still, these are the ones in the families that possibly are the most wounded. They cannot see how their behavior hurts someone because they are so hurt themselves that they inflict pain on anyone connected to them. I have witnessed compulsive behavior and have been involved in it. I have been that family member that responds to something that was said in a negative way and thwarted an angry response toward the person who said it. I have a right to say it was learned behavior, but even if that is true, I give up that right to blame someone else in order to be healthy. To rid yourself of compulsive behavior, you release your need to blame, and you welcome the chance to heal. You rid yourself of a need to justify your actions and you know the only way to change for the better, is to accept whatever criticisms that come with change.

I thought I was healed and one day while at work, a co-worker was having a bad day. It appeared as if she was giving me the cold shoulder so in my compulsiveness, I reacted to her the same way I perceived she had acted towards me. The next day, once she felt better, she tried to approach me with conversation. I was just as short with her as she was with me the day before. I felt justified in my behavior until another co-worker brought something to my attention. She reminded me of a day that I was short with her, not because I was having a bad day, but we were discussing a customer that had rubbed me the wrong way. She had the customer on the phone and saw my notes and was asking me about our previous conversation. As soon as she said the customer's name, I responded negatively. Though it was not toward her, she said my response still rubbed her the wrong way.

I never knew I had offended her in any way because when I did speak to her again, she chose to let bygones be bygones, and she talked to me. It was only until she saw how I was treating the other co-worker did she bring the situation to my attention. This sounds like the servant in the Bible that refused to forgive another servant's debt after his was forgiven. We tend to want something that we refuse to give. Compulsive behavior does not give us the right to judge the compulsiveness of someone else. Healthy thinking is when you hear the constructive criticism of others and instead of justifying misbehavior, you yield to correction. In dysfunctional families, no one likes to yield. Everyone wants to hold on to their right to be hurt without acknowledging the hurt of someone else. This is the compulsive effect.

The Addictive Personality Effect

When family dynamics are thwarted, those with addictive personalities find ways to self-medicate their pain. According to American Addiction Centers, there are traits that can be recognized in people who have a higher risk of becoming addicted to substances. People with this high addiction risk include those who are:

- Related to others who have developed addiction
- Experiencing other mental health disorders
- Adventurous and risk-taking
- Disconnected and cautious
- Obsessive and compulsive
- Apathetic
- Unable to self-regulate

Some of these risks correlate to the previous effect which is compulsive. Careful attention should be paid to the fact that each of these effects overlap one another. One of the biggest effects of dysfunctional families is alcoholism and addiction.

As a child, I had a parent and several other family members that participated in active addiction. I also had friends whose parents and other family members participated in active addiction. In families where abuse is present, normally substance abuse

Crooked Trees: Building on a Fragile Foundation

follows. I know people who have been sexually abused and to self-medicate the pain of that abuse, they started to smoke marijuana. Though they believe that smoking marijuana is not as bad as what they consider the harder substances, they fail to see that they still are addicts-just functioning addicts. I seldom know people who do not have at least one substance abuser in their family. The American Society of Addiction Medicine (ASAM) defines addiction as a prolonged disease of the brain, which involved changes to the reward centers, leading to alterations in behaviors, drive, retention, and cognition. In reflecting back to the compulsive effect, a person with addictive personality has a problem controlling their impulses, sound familiar? This is the kind of person that made sudden moves with little to no thought as to how it will affect themselves or others.

I have watched hours of video surrounding substance abuse, often hearing stories of the dysfunction that led to self-medication. After years of punishment, somehow the substance abuser finds a way to abuse themselves. How many people can we save from addiction if families would just get the help they need from the beginning? If you have an adult that went through years of molestation from various family members, how can you judge the act without judging the cause? Dysfunction has its own kind of tree, like the family tree. There are roots of pain that run deep. As you get to the branches, you cannot help but to see the various ailments that result from unresolved issues. Addiction is not just limited to illegal substances, it extends to food, alcohol, shopping, social media, sex, gambling, smoking, etc. Every article I have read concerning addictive personalities refer to compulsive behavior. How much of this behavior stems from secrets within the family that a person was forbidden to tell? Dr. Allen Lang confirms a correlation between addiction and personality. According to Bartleby.com, family influences our personality, behavior, beliefs, and values. If we combine the two statements, there is a correlation between addiction and family influences.

Crooked Trees: Building on a Fragile Foundation

Not everyone has an addictive personality. Therefore, the power of using substances for self-medication is not as enticing. But there are victims of substance abuse that are also victims of the effects of family dysfunction. After speaking to several recovering substance abusers, each time when asked the question of what led them to drug use, a situation dealing with childhood and family was the culprit. A direct quotation of one of these conversations is as follows:

"Before I became ten years old, I had already been molested. By the age of twenty, I had been molested again. I began to question my existence along with my purpose for living. There were times when I felt like nothing because of the pain that my family never addressed as a result of this abuse. I began taking drugs to help me wake up. Drugs began to give me a reason for living. It may not have been the best reason to live, but at least it kept me alive."

The story continued with each interview. As I asked several people why, the answer, though in different words always reverted to pain. I had another story from someone struggling with substance abuse,

"I use drugs to ease the pain of the past...growing up with an absent father and my mom on drugs put me in a bad place. I began selling drugs to get what other kids had, and I began using drugs to forget why I was selling drugs."

Repeatedly, I kept hearing how using drugs was a cover up for pain.

The Need for Control Effect

Many relationships are challenged by the need for control. Funny thing is, I have seen a need for control not only in personal relationships but in professional relationships as well. According to Wikipedia, there is a personality disorder that demonstrates a need to control. This personality is obsessive-compulsive disorder which gives reference to previous effects discussed in this chapter. With

Crooked Trees: Building on a Fragile Foundation

obsessive-compulsive disorder, a person has a need to for orderliness, perfectionism, excessive attention to details, mental and interpersonal control, at the expense of flexibility, and openness to experience. With a need to control, many may find it very difficult to relax which in some cases stem back to addictive personality effect and substance abuse. When life deals a blow of circumstances that one cannot control, it can lead to them severely controlling the things in life that they can control.

In an article in Psychology today written by Sean Grover *L.C.S.W* on November 30, 2017, he speaks of controlling personalities. The article, entitled, *"Do You Have a Controlling Personality?"* He asks a few underlying questions; *Do you feel betrayed when others don't do what you want? Do you wrestle with trusting people? Do you have a history of combative relationships?* What people fail to realize is that with their need to control, they are the common denominator to all their failed relationships. In this same article, the author speaks about the challenges that this kind of behavior can cause; *escalating conflicts (chronic conflict effect), decreasing trust, and ongoing bickering (chronic conflict effect).* In the case where I was a victim of abuse, my abuser was very controlling. He told me whether I could go anywhere, speak on the phone, what I could and could not wear and so on. The relationship did not begin this way, but once I fell in love with him, he started to show his true colors. There was nothing I could do without his permission, and if I attempted to do anything I wanted to do, it would result in a physical altercation.

Because I was abused, I began to have a problem with authority. If the authority was subtle, I could deal with it, but if it came off as aggressive- I had a problem with it. I had a job once where a manager wanted me to work overtime. Overtime was not mandatory. Another area was offering overtime and the money I made from my previous department was much easier than the overtime in my present department. He kept telling me to work the overtime, but I continued to refuse because it was not mandatory. He was upset and, in his attempting to force me, it landed us both

Crooked Trees: Building on a Fragile Foundation

in Human Resources. In getting back to the article mentioned above, it states that people with controlling tendencies are frequently successful in their careers. It is my belief that they are successful at the expense of others. I have a few family members that are very successful entrepreneurs but working for them has been very demanding.

I had a cousin once to tell me that she would always be on her daughter about her lack of cleaning the house. Her daughter said to her, *"It is not that I do not clean, I just don't clean like you."* How many of us have been in families that wanted to control us? Families that did not just offer advice, they made you seem like you had no other choice but to do what they asked or else? In a conversation with my mom, she told me of a feeling of control. In this case, it appears to be the best solution, but it still had an adverse reaction. My grandmother died when my mom was fourteen years old. My mom is the eldest of six children and when her mom died, she felt she was made to be responsible for her younger siblings. She says, *"I was made to be the wife without the responsibility of intimacy."* She explained it as having to do everything a wife had to do, but please my grandfather intimately. He never handled any of his children in a sexually inappropriate manner. Still she felt like she went from child to wife at the age of fourteen. When she graduated high school and wanted to accept a track scholarship, my grandfather would not allow her to. She had to stay home and continue to raise the children.

She later revealed that she married my father, so she could get away from this life that she did not ask for. I have talked to so many women who have admitted that they got married to leave home. If home was unhealthy, they found the first man willing to make them a wife, and they left. I do not know what led my abuser to being controlling. I know that two of his sisters were married at the age of sixteen, but like any other family there was a lot of generational history that was left untold. I know my daughter's grandmother told me that her father raised them because her mother left, but those were the only details I received. In an article

Crooked Trees: Building on a Fragile Foundation

in Power of Positivity, Dr. Mai Stafford says, *"By contrast, psychological control can limit a child's independence and leave them less able to regulate their own behavior."* In the very first sentence of the article it states, *"Families can go from being present, to being too present."* What did she mean by this? During my first marriage, I was told by one of my family members, *"You graduated from Samford University and you married someone who can barely comprehend."* I know my family has good intentions, but the person who told me this was married to a university scholar and their mental aptitude was barely the equivalent.

I grew up watching many members of my family control their children, spouses, and each other. One of my family members who is now deceased felt like he could never please his father. This caused him a great deal of stress and there were times he would confide with me about his concerns. I have witnessed family members tell people who they can and cannot date even in instances where their concerns were valid. I have even seen this control from my family spill over into their careers where their leadership of other people have been dysfunctional. Levels of control such as this, lead to areas of codependency. This codependency can lead to substance abuse but can also lead to unhealthy relationships. Controlling relationships with parents can lead to co-dependent relationships with others. I know of a young man who grew up in a controlling situation where it was more about control than showing love. Now, it appears that this young man looks for love in sex and multiple relationships. No matter how volatile the relationship is, he stays for as long as he can, and even when it is dissolved, he quickly finds another volatile relationship to enter.

While in the relationship with my abuser, I noticed that if any of his mother's children did not align with what she would say, she would change her will. I do not know the true number of times that will was changed. All I know is that every couple of months, she would let me know who her current beneficiary was. I have another family member that was so displeased with one of his kids that he did the same thing. I can speak of another family member that has changed their beneficiary from me, to another family member, and so on. Thing is, I am sure that we believe ourselves to be healthy individuals. We can appear justified in our actions because after all it is our money to do as we please, but how can we see these decisions without acknowledging a level of dysfunction? In order to help set someone free, I would like to show the differences between a healthy family and a controlling family. Maybe with these details, someone will be able to realize that there is a need to re-evaluate their actions.

In healthy families, a parent's love is not based on a child's actions. The love in this parent/child relationship is not sporadic, but consistent. This love is not filled with constant ridicule and the children can get the proper nurturing just like the nourishment in the tree. With controlling families, a parent's love is conditional. I will only love you if you please me. If you fail to please me, I will relinquish my rewards and support. In healthy families, children are valued. You care for them because that is your duty as a parent. But in dysfunctional families, children are your property just like slaves, to do with as you please. I am not saying that you cannot discipline a child for inappropriate behavior. Discipline such as a time out, weekly grounding, or some other chastisement for misbehavior, but not where a child is reprimanded for not adding up to some unrealistic expectations. Unrealistic expectations like, not wanting to help with tuition because a child did not attend the school you always desired to attend. Failure to offer financial assistance because they went to the school of their choice. Parents who disown a child because of an untraditional or unbiblical sexual preference fall into this category.

In controlling families, children are raised to mimic the things their parents have decided for their lives. These are the children that are made to be in the band though they prefer art. Those who are made to major in medicine when they desire theatre. While those in a healthy family are given the freedom to choose their own area of interests without fear of being ridiculed.

Crooked Trees: Building on a Fragile Foundation

With controlling families, feedback is discouraged; while in healthy families, children are asked about their concerns during dinner. Controlling families suffer dogmatic schisms where the parents only want what they want without being open-minded about anything that the child may desire. The communication between parent and child comes across like it's my way or the highway instead of finding a suitable compromise. I will never forget when my child wanted to go to cosmetology school. Of course, I wish she had picked the entire college experience-especially since I never stayed on campus; but I looked at the fact that trades offer a smaller tuition and a greater chance of her working in her field.

Parenting should never be presented to a child in a manner of the taskmaster vs. the slave. A child should never feel like their faults are constantly criticized. Parenting should have patience where a parent learns to resolve conflict properly to avoid the chronic conflict effect. I have mentioned to my child on several occasions that just because I am mom does not mean I am always right. I have given her permission to come talk to me when she feels like she has been wronged. I told her it is not what she says, but how she says it. If she is respectful in her approach, I do not mind her telling me if she feels like I have done something she is not pleased with. Even in times where I have preferred that she has dated someone differently, I still know that she has the final say. I would rather she date who she wants feeling open enough to ask my opinion about things than I drive her away and not be able to guide her along the way. As parents, we keep our kids closer to us when we can be open about their decisions and trust that we raised them well enough to know when a change needs to be made.

It's okay to want what's best for your children, but do not allow unhealthy thinking to cause you to wage an unnecessary war. Never badger a child with unrealistic expectations. Never ask a child to become something that was impossible for you to become and never ask them to accomplish things that you did not accomplish. Healthy parenting encourages your child to put their best foot forward and in their best effort, always be pleased.

Crooked Trees: Building on a Fragile Foundation

Healthy parenting deals with training a child just like an employer trains a new employee, and when mistakes are made submit feasible solutions. Healthy parenting accepts responsibility for the parts you have played in your child's upbringing, knowing when some things are your fault. As a parent, know when to apologize and know when to press. This is not limited just to parenting, there can also be controlling siblings and other family members. Being healthy means you know when to back off. Even if you are filled with dysfunction from a difficult childhood, learn to get help by following healthy boundaries.

The Emotionally Distant Effect

When you find a person that is emotionally distant, this too, can be a coping mechanism. Just as we discussed self-medication with substance abuse, one can also self-medicate with emotional detachment. I can find myself in each of the effects, some I have overcome, and others continue to be a process. Even with the writing of this book, I believe there is still residual negative behavior learned as a child. Emotional distancing is a sign that one has not fully healed. It is a protective mechanism that causes one to be unable to give any relationship their all. As a child, dysfunction caused a lot of disappointment and feelings of being let down from people who were supposed to love me. Prior to facing emotional distancing, I found myself looking for love in all the wrong places.

A person can chase love so much that eventually the pain of rejection causes them to emotionally shut down. I remember being the young lady that would dive in head first and at the first sign of trouble, I would unconsciously shut down. Eventually, I became the young lady that was able to have an intimate relationship with someone that I did not love. My heart had hardened, and I did not even realize the day it began. How many people enter relationships, promising a lifelong commitment, and shut down as soon as they second guess this commitment? How many people enter relationships for the wrong reasons and when they feel that they are not getting what they have signed up for, they change their minds? How many people stay in relationships physically, but mentally their minds are a million miles away? In my opinion, Christians and those of other religions, tend to stay in unhealthy relationships in the name of their God.

I know several people whose marriages have failed because of emotional distancing. It is amazing how a man can marry the woman of his dreams, only to allow the pain of his past to cause him to dissociate himself from her. She is left wondering what she has done wrong, without realizing it is something he is trying to protect himself from. As a wife, you can be loyal, but in the heat of an argument you could have said something that reminded him of the pain of his last relationship and now because of an unresolved conflict in the past, he has emotionally separated himself from his wife. Have you witnessed a person who will not put their all into any relationship? You watch them interact with their spouse, siblings, parents, co-workers, and so many others. Yet, they are unable to forge a close bond with anyone. Emotional distancing is not easily resolved because people have buried the pain of their past and are no longer in touch with the events that made them distant in the first place.

In my family, you could confide in one person- only to find that the entire family knew what was said. How did you find out, as soon as someone got mad at someone else, they would tell you all your secrets that were repeated? No matter how many times you needed someone to talk to in private, anything shared amongst my family would find a leak. Even if you were on the listening end and offered suggestions for a solution, you would find that once the conversation was repeated the only part brought to light is what you said. Betrayal leads to emotional distancing. When you feel like the only way to protect you is to not care. Just like one with an addiction, the person who is emotionally distant has found a way to protect themselves. They are like a computer that is overloaded, emotionally they have crashed. Too many let downs have caused them to not expect anything else out of a person but disappointment. Now, relationships become routine and they stick with them because they have adapted to dysfunction.

Emotional distancing is subtle. It happens a little at a time, with each painful event in life, until it is full blown, and you fail to see when it attached itself to you. With this effect, love ones can become casualties of war. A person could try so many times to remedy a relationship and get tired due to another's resistance. This is not true just for a marriage, it is true for other relationships in the bloodline. With marriages, a wife can ask a husband to go to counseling. She can try to communicate with her spouse and ask the opinions of others. If she sees that the issue is not being resolved, she will detach herself emotionally for fear of further hurt. Husbands can make efforts to get better and if they feel their wife is never satisfied, they can emotionally detach themselves for fear of being defeated. Children can emotionally detach themselves from parents, siblings from siblings; emotional detachments are just another method of self-medication.

There are women who chose to have babies that resulted from rape or incest, and they are emotionally distant towards those children. As stated previously, when you are emotionally distant, you are not healed. It is difficult to notice your lack of healing because so many others in your circle look just like you. How do you know what healthy looks like if you do not know anyone who is healthy? Even when one may attend therapy, it is hard to grasp the thought of being healthy without knowing someone who is. When I was a child, what I heard in therapy were a whole lot of myths. I would go and learn all these coping mechanisms just to enter back into my world of dysfunction. The thing I agree with most about drug recovery is them telling a newcomer to change their people, places, and things. This is wonderful for an adult who can begin again, but what about a child who has yet to find their independence. The pain of their environment tends to bear such a burden on their hearts that a great number of them become emotionally distant. This results in the breakdown we see in our communities and crime is the end result.

Crooked Trees: Building on a Fragile Foundation

My favorite saying once I made the decision to get better was this, "As a child I had no say in living in dysfunction, but as an adult- I do." I refuse to continue in the way of dysfunction. I am allergic to it and I despise it. Thing is, just because I have begun a journey of emotional recovery does not mean that those closest to me are ready to join me. The biggest challenge of marriages is when one spouse wants help and the other spouse feels like everything is okay. Marriages fail time in and time out because of the effects of dysfunction. One of the biggest injustices to marriage is a dysfunctional husband expecting a wounded wife to submit to even more dysfunction. This results in the chaotic conflict effect because the marriage continues to suffer due to lack of a resolution. Either the wife or husband has had enough, and they begin to retreat to the balcony of their minds. They begin to find the wrong kind of coping mechanisms and they withdraw emotionally from the relationship but still remain their physically. Marriages suffer when the individuals in the marriage refuse to get healthy for themselves and as a result their mates and children suffer.

In this journey to become a subject matter expert in dysfunction, I have met people who my heart goes out to. People who hurt people, administer this hurt as a result of emotional distancing. If you can devalue the relationship in your mind, you are not emotionally attached enough to care what the outcome of the relationship will be. Women who encounter several hurtful relationships with men who are wounded often find themselves victims of emotional distancing. When you distance yourself emotionally, you seldom admit wrongdoing? Somehow you find a way to make yourself a victim and you seldom see the part you play in conflict. In order that we migrate back into healthy households, we must first become healthy ourselves. I have been on the receiving end of counseling and will never be close minded about receiving the right kind of help. We cannot limit our resources by feeling like we should keep our dysfunction secret. That is a learned behavior and when we refuse help, we hurt ourselves and those who relate to us. Talking to someone about your problems is

Crooked Trees: Building on a Fragile Foundation

not airing out your dirty laundry, it is about finding coping mechanisms and conflict resolution. When we fall out with our love ones, we should know steps to take to resolve the issue. We cannot just start back speaking and feel that is enough. Emotional distancing comes from unresolved conflict. Unresolved conflict is a wound that has not healed and whenever the wound is hit and reinjured, it reminds us why we distanced ourselves in the first place.

There are several roles in family dynamics. The effects listed above are in my own words and come from things that I see fit to stress in writing this book. Therefore, these may be terms that have yet to be adopted as valid but demonstrate the things I have researched and can identify with. However, the roles I am about to mention are the roles that are taught, documented and accepted as teaching mechanisms for common family roles. The first role is the hero. The hero is known as the do-gooder. This is the child that is more responsible and a very high achiever. The hero looks to accomplishments to avoid feelings of inadequacy. As a child, I was a hero. I made the perfect grades hoping it would gain the attention of my parents who had problems of their own. I would enter the spelling bee each year and strive to learn as many words as I could. I had to prove myself worthy of my parents love, so I had to accomplish one good thing in school after another. I excelled in basketball and participated in as much as I could to make sure my parents saw who I thought I needed to be.

Another role is the rescuer. The rescuer is the problem solver of the family, always looking for a solution to all problems. When my parents were struggling financially, I got a job to take care of myself, so they would not have to worry or strain by taking care of me. I took on the title of rescuer often giving my parents money when they fell short on bills. I would always step in to take up for someone else, literally getting into physical altercations with other family members who I felt had been wronged. Another role is the mediator, like the rescuer, because the mediator strives to keep peace within the family. There have been times when I have made effort to contact someone concerning a family dispute and even investigated group counseling to get my family to come together. As much as I research, resources show as much as a rescuer or mediator thinks they have a drive to help others, facts show that this person may be doing all this because of something dysfunctional within themselves.

The scapegoat of the family is the person the family feels needs the most help. This is the person in the family that gave in to their addictive personality and needs treatment. This is the person that is evidence that there is a problem within the family. This person normally has a great sense of humor and is willing to be honest and close to their feelings. The switchboard is the information center of the entire family. They are connected and tend to know everything going on within the family, good and bad. The power broker is the person that can categorize the stages of the family, mostly putting themselves at the top. This is the family member who only feels secure with being in control of others and the atmosphere that surrounds them. The lost child is the obedient, but passive child. This child stays out of the way and tries hard to avoid being the problem. The clown is like the class clown because this person knows there are issues, feels the effects of those issues, but hide their true feelings to prove that everything is okay.

The cheerleader is the person who provides support and encouragement to others, which in my healthier state is a role I play well. Before hand I was the rescuer, focusing more on the needs of others than my own. The cheerleader has a healthy balance between helping others in the family and themselves. The nurturer provides emotional support. Until this day, I cannot be sure that my family has this role to be played out in full. The nurturer creates safety and focuses on meeting everyone's emotional needs. The thinker always approaches each circumstance with a level of reasoning. This person can give various perspectives while allowing others to see how another person may feel. Last is the truthteller. This is the person that will tell the family what they see to be true

Crooked Trees: Building on a Fragile Foundation

without sugar coating it. If the family is messed up, they are not afraid to say it, and their delivery of the information may not always be tasteful. These roles may help us dig deeper into our dysfunction, seeing how we relate to these roles help us to overcome things that may be hindering us individually and corporately.

These are the effects and roles of dysfunction within a family. These are the red flags that detail the signs of a shaky foundation. If a reader can identify with any of the details listed above in this chapter, it shows a need for healing to take place in their lives. I have found that in my making this decision, the entire family did not follow me at once, but others followed suit. I have received texts where family members have identified the process of healing in my life. They have commended me even though they have yet to start the process for themselves. The communication concerning my healing shows me that they are paying attention and eventually their time will come. In jail ministry, I relate every subject matter in the curriculum to dysfunction. After a subject is taught in detail, I take a personal event in my life and apply it to the scripture. At times, I can see an inmate who appears uninterested look up when they hear my tales of family dysfunction. Each one of us have the power on the inside to be great, we just need to uncover that greatness by shoveling off the layers of dysfunction.

Each of the effects mentioned above are toxic, meaning, the contents of the family dynamics have contributed to the dysfunction of everyone that is connected to them. We can dress for success and look the part, but each of these categories show the reason why some of our trees are crooked.

Genesis 3

For Bible readers, it did not take long for dysfunction to enter into God's perfect design. Scholars may argue that God's plan A failed so He went with a plan B. I do not believe God's plan failed. I believe because He allows self-will, we failed, not God. I am always fascinated by the old Walgreen's commercials that say, "In a perfect world we have this…but for everything else, there is a Walgreen's." This is my concept for God's design. In a perfect world, we have a world without sin, but since we don't, there is God. Because we are a failed system, God puts in place a divine comeback. He did not create us to fail, it is our dual citizenship that opens a port for the enemy. Anything dealing with flesh has the possibility of falling, which is why God combined our imperfections with His perfection. Humanity has the chance of falling because we tend to make decisions and act off of emotions. The enemy cannot infiltrate a perfect deity, but he can wiggle his way into the portal of our humanness.

We all know the story of Adam and Eve. As long as they walk in their perfection part of the family, they are able to meet with God in the garden during the cool of the day. As long as they are healthy, their world has no evidence of decay. It is the divine part of their citizenship which allows them to be in the presence of God without needing a mediator to stand in the gap for them. The first sign of a breakdown in family dynamics is when Eve is approached by the serpent. Once Eve is tricked into eating the forbidden fruit, we see where the peace of creation is now disturbed. This is the beginning of dysfunction for the inhabitants of the Kingdom of God. After Genesis three, God starts the process of re-establishing His perfect Kingdom. Let's break down the story of the fall and see in what ways can we apply it to our own families. Genesis three shows Satan entering God's perfect design for our lives. The garden is a place of peace and serenity and houses everything that Adam and Eve needs for everyday living.

Crooked Trees: Building on a Fragile Foundation

His plan all along is to break down the family dynamics of what God created. With the seduction of the forbidden fruit, the antagonist enters the scene, and chaos enters as one of the obstacles within the family. Because God is a divine deity, Satan cannot curse or impose his will on God's chosen people, but he can entice them to give up their divine positions themselves. Therefore, with Eve having everything that she needs right before her, the little voice in her ear still entices her to want more. Sin separates us from God, the enemy had to put a wedge between man and their master. How many times are our members at war with themselves? The divine factor of our chemical makeup battling against our flesh. Without resistance, Eve allows the enemy to twist God's words and starts a seduction between her and the fruit. My opinion is the only way that the serpent could entice Eve with the fruit is if secretly she wanted to taste it anyway. Any sin I have found myself entangled with always started with thoughts in my mind first. Though never mentioned, I want to introduce the fact that Eve was toying with eating the fruit long before the serpent presented this thought to her.

Isn't it amazing that Eve was near the tree in the first place, but distant from her husband? If we are near something that is forbidden, this is evidence it is on our minds. The enemy is sure to come after the weakest link when it comes to sabotaging the plan of God for our families. He's had a strategy from day number one and we give in to his devices over and over again. We all know right from wrong, but we give in to the compulsiveness within us without fighting to do things that bring about more healthy outcomes. Could it be that Eve failed because she did not hear God say it for herself? Could it be that this is second-hand information given by Adam? Still, Eve has become one with Adam; made from his rib and should have trusted his words enough to know better. Solitude has taken out many. It is when we find ourselves alone that we tend to give in to the enemy's devices. Proverbs 4:14-15 states, *"Do not set foot on the path of the wicked or walk in the way of evildoers...Avoid it, do not travel on it; turn from it and go on your way (New*

Crooked Trees: Building on a Fragile Foundation

International Version)." Satan tempts Eve because he knows that through her, he can get to Adam.

Deceit begins with misinterpretation of the command. Surely God understands that there is no way you can follow every command of the Bible, after all we are only human right? How many times have we fallen because we tend to walk through questions in our minds of what God intended His word to say? The fruit is given to Adam, and though he knows it is wrong, he also takes, and he eats. The first test of obedience and we fail. There are times when we fall as a result of who we are connected to. We yield out of love, confusion, and other things and find ourselves justifying why we disobey God. Disobedience is the beginning of dysfunction. This is not the will of God and when we go against the grain, there are consequences. Let's go into the consequences of sin in accordance with Genesis three and see how we can contrast sin with dysfunction. Prior to the fall, Adam and Eve willingly meet with God in the cool of the day. After the fall, they realize they are naked and become ashamed. In dysfunction, how many times do we feel uncovered and are ashamed of what we have done? We were not created to disobey God, but because of free will, disobedience is possible.

God shows up at the allotted time of the day and as He calls for them, they are not willing to present themselves. Now, they come before God and tell Him, *"We were afraid because we are naked."* God begins the dialogue with them, *"How do you know you are naked?"* The man immediately begins to blame. The parallels between the fall and dysfunction, how many times do we place blame on others for how we are? The blame can be true, but could we have stopped our behavior? Could we have stopped our destructive behavior even though someone contributed to the reason why we want to act out? God then asks the woman what she has done. The generational behavior begins, Adam, the head of the family blames Eve, and in return she blames the serpent. Can you look throughout your family and see patterns of sin that many of you have in common? Do you believe at the time, that both

Crooked Trees: Building on a Fragile Foundation

Adam and Eve, realize they are shifting blame? God reveals the consequences, starting with the last one to be blamed. He tells the serpent, *"Because you have done this, you are cursed above all cattle, and above every beast of the field; upon thy belly shall you go, and dust shall thou eat all of the days of your life.* Blame does not limit the consequences of the participants involved. Everyone involved in disobedience contribute to the dysfunction that lies ahead.

God continues, *"And I will put enmity between thee and the woman, and between your seed and her seed; it shall bruise your head and you shall bruise his heel."* For the part the woman plays, *"I will greatly multiply thy sorrow and thy conception; in sorrow shall you bring forth children; and your desire shall be to your husband, and he shall rule over you."* Adam cannot escape his consequence, *"Because you have yielded to your wife's commands and have also eaten of the tree of which I told you not to eat, cursed is the ground for your sake...in sorrow shall you eat of it all the days of your life."* He continues, *"Thorns and thistles shall it bring forth to you, and you shall eat the herb of the field...in the sweat of your face shall you eat bread, till you return unto the ground; for out of it were you taken: for dust you are and unto dust you shall return."*

It is in Genesis three that we see that no matter what brings us to our disobedience, it will not exempt us from its consequences. This means even if we are sexually assaulted or wronged, if we continue in disobedience, we have our consequences as well. This does not eliminate the fact that you have been violated, it just shows that if we continue in the sins of our forefathers, we can face the same or similar consequences. Prior to the fall, Adam is given the job of tending the land. Now, the same land he is supposed to tend is now cursed because of his action. It seems like a stiff penalty, but disobedience is defined the same way no matter how great or small. Where does our story begin? I am not asking where our genealogy began, I am asking where did our dysfunction begin? Can our parents sit down and explain to us some things about dysfunction? If they are no longer here with us, do we have other

Crooked Trees: Building on a Fragile Foundation

family members that know something that can shed revelation on what is wrong with our foundation? Would it make a difference to know why some fathers were alcoholic and abusive? Would it help to know that the reason some mothers are promiscuous is because a family friend touched her inappropriately?

God then makes provision for Adam and Eve. He makes coats of skin and clothes them. Now, man is no longer in his divine position of fellowshipping with God on a face to face basis. Where they met in the garden in the cool of the day, now man is exiled from the garden. To make sure they are no longer able to enter into the holy place, God places Cherubim's at the east of the garden. He also places a flaming sword which turned every way to keep the way of the tree of life. What is the tale of our personal Genesis three? Sites like Ancestry.Com are so exciting because it gives us a glimpse into who we are. It tells us who we are connected to. Still, it does not reveal to us our secrets. As I stated in the beginning, I know my great-grandmother's name and I hear stories about her, but I seldom hear stories about my great-grandfather or other husbands. Every family reunion shirt I have shows we derive from my great-grandmother. My Genesis three experience will help me understand me. It will help me know what contributed to my family's shaky foundation. My grandfather being well respected in our community. He was my number one supporter and my relationship was solid. Before he matured, what made him beat my grandmother?

What made members of my family take to a life of stealing and other illegal activity? Was it the fact that my great-grandmother was desperate to take care of her children on her own? What about my paternal grandfather, what made him abuse both my grandmother and his own children to a point of shooting one of his sons in the head? Family secrets; things so painful that no one wants to speak about them. But, when I find myself being abused, no one can understand why I would submit myself to these things. Could it have been that a conversation with my grandmother could have been what I needed? Could that have

Crooked Trees: Building on a Fragile Foundation

helped me to not feel so alone? I did speak with her once, but for sake of time, our conversation about abuse was limited. After all, mothers want to protect the image of their husbands. Just as my paternal grandmother protected the reputation of my grandfather, my father felt there was no need to discuss his childhood with me. As we continue to read pass Genesis three, we find that the disobedience of the parents led to dysfunction in the lives of the sons. The effects of the fall of Genesis three leads to brother killing brother due to envy concerning sacrifice. The effects of the fall cause us to have to work for what was once free. Sin moves us out of position and now we fellowship with God in faith instead of being able to be face to face with Him in the garden.

How many Cain and Abel stories do we have in modern day time? In my family, both sides, I have known siblings to fight against siblings. Not only do we hear stories of siblings who have killed one another, we also hear of children who have killed their families. Our families are not beyond help if we stop trying to be the face of perfect family dynamics when we know we are not perfect. If you have a family where father and mother remain together, raising children with a lot of love, but teaching them hate of another race; that is dysfunction. The family dynamics of the household may have been solid, but if children can distance themselves emotionally from another because of the color of their skin; that is dysfunction. If parents remain together, loving on their children, but not each other; that is dysfunction. This dysfunction causes a breakdown in the foundation of the family. Today has become one of the hardest generations to live in, with the hardest descendants to reach, because somewhere we got away from what we stand on. We have so much compulsive behavior that there is chaos everywhere. We introduced sex in the media for money and caused our integrity, values, and morals to become extinct.

What types of family situations are birthed from dysfunction? What are the effects of sin on the rest of creation? One situation birthed from dysfunction is rape or molestation, which I have briefly mentioned. In Genesis 34 we meet Dinah, the

Crooked Trees: Building on a Fragile Foundation

daughter of Jacob and Leah. One day she goes out to visit with other women and Shechem, son of Hamor the Hivite, rapes her. It is only after he rapes her that he goes to his father and asks him to get Dinah for him to marry. Jacob's son replied to the request deceitfully. Which this is the same Jacob that was known as the trickster, who bribed his brother Esau for his birthright, and in return was tricked by Laban, Leah's father for her hand in marriage instead of Rachel. Now, his sons are being equally deceitful in an attempt to see revenge for their sister's rape. They tell Hamor, we cannot give our sister in marriage to someone who is not circumcised. We will enter into agreement with you on one condition only, that all of your males become circumcised. Each of the male Hivites yielded at the request and while they were still in pain, Simeon and Levi, took their swords, attacked the city, and killed each of the males.

I am sure like Adam and Eve, Simeon and Levi felt justified. Why would they kill the males, because they raped our sister? Why did Adam eat the fruit, because Eve gave it to him? Why did Eve eat the fruit, because the serpent gave it to her? Can you see how dysfunction brings about justification through blame? Deuteronomy 22:28-29 states, *"If a man happens to meet a virgin who is not pledged to be married and rapes her and they are discovered, he shall pay her father fifty shekels of silver...He must marry the young woman, for he has violated her. He can never divorce her as long as he lives."* I did not mention this scripture to justify rape, I only wanted to show evidence that this kind of behavior existed during biblical times. Just like with Dinah, disobedience causes one to act on compulsive thoughts with no regards as to how their behavior negatively impacts someone else. One day while shopping in a Christian bookstore I saw this quote, *"Sin always sees the bait but is blind to the hook."* How many times do we partake in sin due to instant gratification while ignoring its long-term effect? Shechem went after what he wanted without realizing what it would cost him and his family. How many things have we done without realizing the destruction it will bring about in our house?

Crooked Trees: Building on a Fragile Foundation

Just as in biblical times, this generation has become enlightened with a boatload of sin. I believe a lot of parents became so wounded that they vowed to never raise their children like they were raised. We started to raise children based on our painful experiences and in rebellion we refused to continue with the rules that were established before us. Have you noticed that there are less marriages than there were when we were children? Children are coming from broken homes as if this is supposed to be the norm. If God did not ordain family, why would he say that it was not good for man to be alone? Why would he put Adam to sleep and after taking a rib from his body, create Eve? Why would there be several references to husband and wife commanding them to be fruitful and multiply? Even in cases of homosexuality, how can this be God's designed plan if two of the same sex are unable to procreate? Pain has been around a long time and has resulted in us abandoning our seed emotionally. We have children in foster care because those who should be taking care of them could not hold up to their parental obligations. You hear people ask, "How can God let this happen?" God is never to blame just like Eve could not blame the serpent, and Adam could not blame Eve. We cannot blame God because during creation, He gave us free-will. How many things have we done that we were not supposed to do, but we did them anyway? Healthy people do not inflict pain. Healthy people do not abandon households, nor do they molest children. Healthy people do not emotionally distance themselves from those they are supposed to love. They do not use drugs, nor do they partake in compulsive behaviors that negatively impact themselves or someone else. We are living in a world filled with pain. What we see today is a result of that pain.

Another dysfunction that resulted in the fall connected with Genesis three is David and Bathsheba. While on the balcony bathing, Bathsheba catches the eye of David and it sparks an affair. As a result of this affair, Bathsheba is now with child. In an attempt to cover up the affair, David has a plan to have her husband Uriah killed. Do we not hear stories of adultery and plots to kills today? As a consequence, to the murder of Uriah, the baby does not make

Crooked Trees: Building on a Fragile Foundation

it. Instance after instance, it appears difficult to find an example of a healthy family after the fall. Still, we see story after story of negative behavior. Even in the faithful, because of this dual citizenship of being part man and part divine, we see tests where humanity wins. Abraham is a patriarch of faith. Even after God promises him a seed, he and Sarah devise a plan that they will rush the plan of God by allowing Abraham to sleep with Hagar. His nephew Lot refuses to leave his perverse surroundings, having to offer his daughters intimately to an angry mob that are after the guest angels in his home. Even after they leave Sodom, the same daughters seduce him after getting him drunk, so they can become pregnant with his seed.

As depressing as all of this sounds, there is a way of escape. If we surrender our will over to God's will and put His commandments into practice, we can start the process of having a better life for ourselves. My number one goal is to introduce one to good health and there may be someone who is not quite ready to yield their lives over to God. Maybe in your unhealthy thinking you cannot grasp the concept of a supreme being, but this still should not deter you from starting the process of getting healthy. I am not limiting a need for God, only allowing the reader the same free-will that God offers in the Bible. In order to be free, you must start a plan to rid yourself of the pain associated with the residue of your past. There are healthy people in this world. They are not completely healthy based on a biblical standard, but they are in a continual process of healing. I am one of these people, but I often get stressed because the people I am connected to always appear to challenge this healing. Dysfunction is so much the new norm that people accept it as a way of life.

There is a book by Gary Chapman called *The Five Love Languages*. This book tells you the different ways people desire to be loved. Though it is a book that mostly deals with marriages, I believe everyone should read this book. In my wounded state, I needed someone to reaffirm their love for me constantly. I had several men to steer clear of me because a relationship with me was too much work. I had a gentleman to tell me one day that I put too much responsibility on him to make me happy. Of course, in my wounded state, I did not understand what he meant. Do you know that it is possible to be too clingy and not even know it? No one should ever want to be under another person all the time so that they can feel loved. I never understood this when I needed this unhealthy affection, but once I became emotionally independent, it became very draining to have someone emotionally dependent on me. Marriages fail because of this emotional dependence. The spouse that is being squeezed for this type of affection feels overwhelmed while the spouse who needs this type of affection feels neglected. It is detrimental that we all work on the only person we have true control to control, and that is ourselves. You can try to control people around you and it may work for a while, but sooner or later, they will find a way to rid themselves of you.

I am sharing these examples to show you that if we feed our flesh more than we feed our spirits, we will not be able to live in harmony. Humanity that has been wounded and continues to be fragile, is unable to live in harmony. We will constantly seek something or someone to make us feel better. We allow our pain to alienate us from God and there is a void so large in our lives that it cannot be filled by any substance or person. When we expect a person to fill our void, it becomes a selfish motive. No one can become everything to someone else. Then, if the person you are placing this responsibility on leaves, you feel even more abandoned than you did before. There is nothing as draining than not being able to breathe in your relationship with another person. The person who is sucking the air out of you makes every hobby of interest you have, other than them, a threat. I remember every move my suitor made, I wanted to make with him. If he wanted to go around his friends, I wanted to go. If he could not spend time with me, I felt sad. Every waking moment surrounded me with thoughts of him.

It sounds very disturbing now. A healthy love is a love where two people are able to stand individually. Why so much

Crooked Trees: Building on a Fragile Foundation

dysfunction in the Bible, because God wants to show us His theme? Throughout the entire message, filled with our disobedience, is God's plan to restore His kingdom. Genesis 1-2 shows a world without sin and until we get to Revelation 21-22, we will not get back to the world that God originally designs. Yes, we are emotionally needy aside from Him. God's word gives us an awareness of our sinfulness and our inability to save ourselves. The reason it is difficult to accept this concept is because in the natural, we have never had someone we can totally depend on. We tend to look at our relationship with God and define it based on our experience with man. No matter how unpleasant life's circumstances are, healing is possible through Him. A healthy family is an attainable goal. You cannot go back and present structure to your past, but you definitely can present structure to your future. I learned from a family member that while in recovery you are asked to not date within the first year. This is an awesome concept to me. Too many times did I rid myself from the pain of one failed relationship by going into another. This never gave me time to stand on my own two feet and overcome any of the obstacles that were necessary for me to choose a more appropriate suitor.

We attack God, blaming Him for all of our failed relationships, but never giving thought to the fact that we made the unhealthy decisions. Do not give up because your family has a shaky foundation. Just know that with each situation within the Bible, God is always willing to restore. Yes, David and Bathsheba lost a son, but they gained another son. Yes, Abraham and Sarah went ahead of God, but they still received Isaac. Trusting God to restore us to our original state is difficult. If the people we see have wreaked havoc in our lives, how can we depend on God who we cannot see to resolve our issues? My faith in God made the healing process possible. It was through His word that I found value and cared enough to no longer be compulsive or to live in chronic chaos. I learned to set boundaries for myself that those who wanted to connect with me had to follow. Families need to come together and properly communicate the things that have them bound. If you ever want to rid a flower bed of weeds, you must pluck the weed from the root. If the root is never addressed, no matter how much you cut it, it will always come back. I once had a mole that was growing through my scalp. I went to the dermatologist and they cut it. Months later, the mole was back. Once while getting my hair done, my stylist was cutting my hair, and in error cut the mole off. Once again, within several months, it grew back. When I went back to the dermatologist, they said they would have to go in and remove it from the root.

Once removed this time, it was stitched up never to return again. If you ever find yourself in the vicious cycle of hurt, it is time that you address the root issue. I believe a substance abuser will have a difficult time remaining clean if they only look to get off of drugs. They can detox and follow the steps, but if they never address the root cause of their addiction, I believe they will fail. If someone is struggling with adultery, they can attempt to remain faithful as much as they can. It is only until they address the need to going outside the marriage, will they successfully give their all to their marriage. Some people commit adultery because they feel unfulfilled in their marriage. Others struggle with lust and because of pornography and other factors; they are dissatisfied with what they have at home. Some have thought in their hearts concerning the other gender and because they devalue them for some reasons or other, they cannot commit to just one. I know men personally who despise their mothers. Therefore, they objectify women. I know women who feel like their husbands are not the man their fathers were, and because of this they look outside the home. At the end of the day, we have a lot of reasons to justify our dysfunction. But it is only until we stop blaming others and accept our part in our behavior, can we overcome the effects of our dysfunction.

Crooked Trees: Building on a Fragile Foundation

 Disobedience is the beginning of dysfunction. This is not the will of God and when we go against the grain, there are consequences.

Generational Behavior

Lamentations 5:7 say, *"Our fathers have sinned, and are not; and we have borne their iniquities."*

I have watched documentaries of women who landed in prison due to substance abuse. During the same documentary, they have mentioned a child that is also in prison for the same reason. In my own family, I have seen siblings be affected by something generational differently. I have seen instances where the parents were addicts and one child will become addicted to a substance while another child will not. One child will drop out of school because of their parent's addiction and the other will excel. Still, at the end of the day, each of them still has their areas of dysfunction. Dysfunction does not just show up inside a family without reason. When someone in the family unlocks the door, sin feels it has a right to enter. None of us can choose our family. We are born into our families without rights to say whether or not we think they are able to provide for us mentally, emotionally, or financially. Fathers who struggle with infidelity that results in a lot of children, tend to have sons with those same issues. The fathers often fail to tell the sons about their problems with infidelity because they are too entangled in it themselves.

While my maternal grandfather abused my grandmother, I did not see this reflected in each of my uncles. Only one seemed to follow in these footsteps and just as my grandfather changed, so did my uncle. While my paternal grandfather abused my grandmother, I did not see instances where my uncles followed in this same behavior. One of my uncles actually moved out of state and started a life of recovery. While my maternal grandfather would drink heavily, two of my mother's siblings chose to never drink and the remainder of them either struggled with alcoholism or substance abuse. While my paternal grandfather would drink heavily, I had two uncles who would drink heavily and remained functional. While my maternal grandfather had a problem with infidelity, I saw several members of my family struggle with infidelity including the grandchildren. I have other aunts and uncles that are not by my biological grandmother and even found that one of my childhood friends was actually one of my aunts. I do not know much about whether or not my paternal grandfather participated in infidelity. The only thing I know about his behavior is alcoholism and abuse.

My mother is open with me about the obstacles she faced in her childhood. I often say that even though I am her firstborn, I am actually her sixth child. My mother admitted that it was a struggle wanting to raise me because she still had animosity toward my grandmother for abandoning her and leaving her to look after her five siblings. When I first came along, she was an outstanding mother. I remember being neatly dressed, hair always combed well, and having everything I needed and wanted. I remember that I was not allowed to use words that I could not spell. If I used a word that she believed I did not know, she would ask me to spell it. If I could not spell it, she would give me a week to learn, and I would have to spell it for her at the end of the week. The only way I could add new words to my vocabulary was to learn how to spell the word I was using. With my report card, I was rewarded faithfully for good grades. I received $5 for each A, $4 for each B and if I was to get a C, I had to pay $1 back. There were not too many times I received a C because of the incentives, I made the honor roll a lot. My childhood started out healthy. I had both parents who were very hardworking. My mother coached both the cheerleaders and the boys' basketball team and attended PTA meetings at my school. She was very involved as a mother and hid her imperfections for a long time until they became too much to bear.

My father was anti-social. He had no friends apart from my mother's friends and went from partying with my mother to yielding his life to God. My father never received phone calls from anyone except my grandmother. His entire life revolved around our household, his job, and his church work. He was Sunday School Superintendent, church custodian, van driver, and a deacon. I learned most of my faith from him. The hardest part of my household after my father's conversion was now, he and my mother had become unequally yoked. Beforehand, they both partied. Now, my mother went out and I was always left home with my father. Being around my mother's family was very challenging. I loved them, but I hated them. I know hate is a very strong word. It was pretty much that I loved the person, but I hated the behavior. I was the oldest grandchild in the state of Alabama on my mother's side. I saw a lot of things that I knew was not healthy, but as a child you learned to not discuss the details of what went on behind closed doors. It was nothing for me to go to a family member's house to go shopping. A day of shopping with my mother was not at the store, it was in a room filled with stolen clothes. It was nothing to go to a family member's house and see a table filled with marijuana waiting to be packaged for sale.

It did not feel bad because we were being looked after. It was only until some of our family members began to get high off of their own products that things began to go awry. Some members graduated from marijuana to cocaine, others to crack cocaine. The true test of family was seeing family members criticize the sins of others without acknowledging the sins of themselves. One of my family members witnessed his mother shot by his father several times. This family member came to live with us, but I never witnessed this family member get additional help, if any to sort out the things in life that he had seen. Another family member, abandoned by a parent on drugs, came to live with us and was removed by authorities and placed in foster care. Other family members, siblings, were relocated after one of their parents successfully recovered from drugs. During this time, we lived with my maternal grandfather and it felt as if I had siblings. Soon after everyone was plucked away one by one, I was left to face life alone without any of my self-defined siblings.

Crooked Trees: Building on a Fragile Foundation

Other generational behavior to follow my family other than abuse, addiction, and infidelity are abortions. Without releasing details, I learned of our struggles with abortion after I had one of my own. I also used my experience to minister to another family member who was not aware of the abortions that came before her own. Additional generational behavior can be poverty, families who are comfortable with living in conditions that do not require much effort. This can include families who live off of assistance and never start the process of independent living. Divorce can be a generational behavior. Mental illness, health issues, and so many other things can also be generational. In my husband's family is a lot of premature death from medical illnesses. They have lost several loved ones to various forms of cancer. Though my husband will never admit the adverse effect these deaths have had on his life, any time I do not feel well, he encourages me to go to the doctor. I have gastrointestinal issues and no matter how much I have seen a doctor and they assure me it's IBS or diverticulosis, he is reminded that once his mother's gall bladder was removed, they found stage four cancer.

I have several male family members that were incarcerated. Though rocky starts, most of my maternal family members follow in the footsteps of my grandfather and tend to steer clear of negative behavior later in life. Though evidence of dysfunction in the form of illegal behavior no longer surfaces, there is still residue concerning what I feel is inherited behavior. It is amazing how people learn to function in dysfunction and are okay with the effects of it. It is amazing how people become okay with not being okay. I watched a documentary on You-Tube titled, "The Family I Had." A young mother is working late one night only to be notified her thirteen-year-old son killed her four-year-old daughter. As the documentary continued, she mentioned that her mom had been acquitted in the murder of her father. Both she and her mom dabbled in drugs and alcohol. Also, the thirteen-year old's dad suffered from a form of schizophrenia. In my opinion, these are all forms of dysfunction brought about by generational behavior. She had taken her mom's word that she did not kill her father, but after what happened with her children, the young mother was no longer sure. She spoke to the arresting officer in her mom's case and found out there was evidence that shows her mom conspired to kill her dad.

My daughter is aware of who her biological father is, but I left before she had a chance to spend a significant amount of time with him. Still, unbeknown to her, she hates funerals and will avoid them at all cost. Her dad is the same way, he did not attend either of his grandparents, his mother's or his daughter's funeral. Her dad loves cartoons and so does she. He is very antisocial and so is she. She is not a people's person, seldom interacts with crowds, is particular about who he converses with, and so is she. He can have an attitude for no reason, and she has told me that she has had times where she has been in a bad mood for no reason. We tend to want to chastise children for certain behavior without getting proper treatment for that behavior. As much as I thought I left in enough time for her to not be affected by his behavior, she still inherited some of it. She is not abusive, physically or verbally. Still, she does not trust people easily and she observes a person closely before she allows them into her personal space. Her paternal uncle attempted to talk to her once at a family gathering and she was very distant. He immediately reprimanded her dad telling him that he has negatively impacted his children.

While watching another documentary, I learned of a mixed family of British descent. A wife, her husband, his son from a previous marriage, and their daughter together lived in Britain. The son began to get into so much legal trouble that they decided to be traveling pub owners. This caused them to not be in a single location for long periods of time. Without realizing the negative affect the traveling had on the kids, they were more concerned about saving their reputation in society instead of getting their son the proper help he needed to deal with his issues. In their traveling, it kept both kids from making stable friendships and other social connections. The son began molesting the daughter due to the isolation of not being able to stay in a community long enough to date. The daughter hid the situation and even when becoming pregnant at the age of twelve, she lied and told her parents and the authorities that she had sex with a young man outside of her school. They never found out the truth until after the son became an adult and killed his live-in girlfriend in front of her children. When he went on the run, he later somehow came back to his mom's and killed one of his nieces by the same sister he had impregnated many years earlier.

Their father had passed away and the stepmom and half sister were afraid of him, still allowing him to come in and out of their lives. The half sister's husband noticed how afraid his wife was of the brother and only after he killed one of their daughter's was the truth found out of how he had molested her and fathered her eldest child. How much of what goes on in our private lives do we hide? What secret demons do we face that keep us imprisoned? How many generational behaviors have we inherited and because we are not aware of their origin, we are too filled with shame to get help for them? I have never been one to use drugs, but I did self-medicate with relationships. I suffered from depression and while the rest of my family as previously mentioned felt that I was the only one, with all of the drug use, there was no way I was the only one. I learned dysfunction as a child, and I accepted it as normal as an adult until I began to get involved with the church and began to desire something better for myself.

I never had a problem with healthy authority, but whenever I came in contact with someone over me that I felt was dysfunctional; my wounds would peep out their ugly heads. I do not like to be in an atmosphere of injustice. I tend to stand up and become very outspoken when I feel like something is unjust. Even as I write this book, I realize that no matter how far I have come, I still have a way to go. Because I grew up in a family where it was nothing for a family member to grab your bottom as a joke, I despise even my husband placing his hand on my bottom. None of my male family members have inappropriately had sexual relations with me, but all of the women in our family are mostly blessed in the gluteus maximus area. Therefore, at every family function there were a number of jokes about my butt while family members would feel on my butt. Even married, when my husband refers to jokes about how he likes my big bottom or wants to touch it, it makes me feel very uneasy. I actually hate people to touch my bottom. I guess I need to start working on what makes me twinge at the sight of a hand coming towards my butt.

It is amazing how much we bring positives and negatives from our childhood to the table. In my current marriage, my husband loves for me to cater to him. He loves having my undivided attention. He believes a woman is to prepare his meal and bring it to him. I started doing it and after a while, it became an inconvenience. I want him to see that because I work the second shift, I no longer feel like preparing his food nor bringing him his plate. I have learned that is something that his mother did for his dad. I also see that even in his mom's passing, his dad's current girlfriend waits on his dad hand and foot. When I try to get my husband to see my perspective concerning this matter, he is unable to see it because this is all he has seen for all of his life. The biggest struggle in our marriage is what we have inherited in our upbringing. How many marriages suffer out of our inability to overcome the flaws of inherited behavior? As adults, we must be able to differentiate between healthy and unhealthy behavior. We have to work through things in life that do not fit. We must take control of our mindsets and make the conscious decision to rid ourselves of any behavior that is not conducive to a healthy lifestyle.

Often times our past is the true reason for the failure of our relationships. We go into relationships without it being well defined and then we want to leave when we have married additional baggage. I am not saying all relationships are worth salvaging. But, no matter how different my husband and my childhoods were, it is not worth a divorce. It just shows me a need why a book of this magnitude needs to be written. Both of us have brought some generational obstacles in our marriage, but as time progresses, we seem to adapt to ways that fit us both. This is one of those moments where for now, we agree to disagree. As I continue to take my counseling courses in school, I will learn some ways to help us resolve various issues. Still, we cannot continue to justify wrongdoing as acceptable behavior. I cannot continue to not cuddle him because I never received affection as a child, and he cannot continue to hold me hostage to chores that his mother was able to accomplish.

Every household cannot be run the same because every household is not set up the same. He is used to a home where his dad received affection from his mom. Therefore, I cannot continue to expect him to accept the fact that my love language has nothing to do with physical touching. Generational behaviors such as this can cause marriages to fail. We are failing at marriage because we have become a society that is accustomed to having things to continue to go as they did in our childhood. The enemy is after marriages because of the benefits of family. We live in a time where the independent wants to do it alone, but there is nothing like having a family all under one roof. Healthy family dynamics can consist of two working parents with enough income to properly tend to their children's needs. They can attend extracurricular activities, outings, and have celebratory occasions. Healthy family dynamics consist of the father being the head, a provider, and disciplinarian while the mother is the helpmate, domestic goddess, and nurturer.

The thing I love most about my husband is his family is his priority. I am not threatened about another woman coming in and destroying his loyalty to me. His loyalty has nothing to do with how I act. There were things in his childhood that he did not agree with and he is loyal because he wants to be. It has nothing to do with me. Therefore, he gives me the security that our relationship is solid and even after an argument, I never get the cold shoulder. He is always willing to allow bygones to be bygones and we never go lengthy periods of time without communicating with one another. Still, there are areas that can be worked out for us both and because I choose to be a better wife, I use resources. It can come in the form of a documentary, sermon, or book. There are times where recordings of Dr. Myles Munroe have helped define some of my shortcomings as a wife. These are the times when I realize that the obstacles in our marriage aren't just him. There are some obstacles that my generational strongholds bring to the table as well. This is where most of us fail as people. We refuse to believe that a method other than the one we have been taught all our lives can be a better way of life.

Our grandparents did not realize that their imperfections would be passed on from them to their children and grandchildren. I bet my grandfather never thought that he would pass on his inherited ailments to his children. I bet his children never thought that they would pass their ailments on to us and my generation never thought that our shortcomings would affect our children. We get so entangled in how we feel and how our childhoods affected us, that we fail to see how our actions affect someone else. No matter how the way we were raised impacted us, it is never too late to begin the journey of getting better. It may not be an easy road, but we all need to start the journey of getting to know ourselves. My mom's knowledge of all of our family issues are limited, but that does not limit me from asking questions. The harder things are to talk about, the more necessary they are for healing. Both of my parents are now in church and open to talking about the more difficult issues. I can ask either of them anything and they will give me an honest response. I have found that with this open line of communication, it is assisting me in my journey to emotional well-being.

I have recently watched a few of the Red Table Talk's with Jada Pinkett Smith. She has discussed the abuse her mom suffered at the hands of her dad along with how she and Will Smith decided to strengthen their marriage. In my journey to healing, I had to first decide to be open to correction. Whenever a person is close minded about their issues, that is a tell-tale sign that they are not going to receive healing. Only a person who is not afraid to look in the mirror and say, "It is I", will receive healing. I will share experience with all who are willing to listen. Even with generational behaviors that I am working hard to overcome, there is still a level of acceptance that I need to have along with accountability that I cannot change until I can accept the possibility that I am not always right. Even in times where I feel like my husband is wrong, I cannot force my journey on him. Believe me, I have tried. The only person I have control over is myself. My journey is not his journey and even if I cannot convince him to change his beliefs that derived from his family dynamics, I can work to change my response to those things.

Nothing in my life has been an easy journey. Still, the reward is set before me, and if I wish to attain the reward, I have to be willing to walk out the process. What is the reward? The reward is knowing that with each step I take toward healthy living, I get happier along the way. It feels good to show up at the family functions and not fall victim to participating in the family chaos. It feels good to walk away and know I did not offend someone. It feels good to know that I do not need alcohol to enjoy myself. It feels good to know that I can accept the fact that conflict does not have to destroy my marriage. It feels good to be at the beginning phase of a distant journey knowing that for once in your life you have made up your mind to live life right. It feels good knowing that life is not always getting the best of me. There were once some stages in my life where the bad in life outscored me often. It feels good knowing that now I win more days than I lose and even on days when I am not at my best, I would rather live than die and try again. Life is beautiful when you learn how to live it. It is beautiful when an obstacle does not make you want to take your life. If we learn how to live properly, we can teach someone else how to overcome some of the things we have in common. I can teach another depressed person how to smile because I overcame depression and learned how to smile.

I once had a friend who doubted my joy. She said there is no way that my life could be perfect all of the time. My life is far

Crooked Trees: Building on a Fragile Foundation

from perfect. Still, the obstacles that I face no longer dictate my view on life. I would rather live with obstacles than to die in defeat. We spend too much time in our lives being ungrateful for what we have while we are in search of something better. Life is like a game of cards. The same hand that I am losing with, a more skilled player can take the same hand and win. My mom loves playing spades. She and most of her siblings are skilled card players. You can group two of the more skilled players together and they can beat everyone who comes to the table until another two players who learned to play the same way comes against them. That is life. Once you learn how to play, no matter how crappy the hand, you are determined to win. Imagine if my husband and I learned to play the game of life together. Imagine if, no matter what cards we are dealt, we have a strategy to defeat all odds to win the game. Some may say, "You do not know my life." I do not have to know the details. All I need to know is whether or not you are ready to start the journey of healing.

I never said that the journey would be easy. Even with everything I have learned, there are still some days where I wonder will I ever complete the journey. I have met ladies in ministry who have been molested and are happy. I have met ladies who have suffered detrimental abuse and have lived to talk about it. I have met ladies who have prostituted themselves for drugs and now have a loving husband, are recovered, and on top of the world. We do not have to accept the flaws of generations that came before us. All we need is a desire to change. I used to be depressed because I allowed my mind to be consumed by painful things. I once had a therapist who told me this, "If most of your childhood memories are bad, make new ones." I told my husband that I have never been to Disney World and I want to go. Don't be surprised if one day while it's hot outside that I just decide to get the hose pipe and play in the water. Once I went to Wal-Mart and purchased myself some Play-Doh, crayons and a coloring book. It appeared to be a phase because once I played with it for a couple of weeks, I no longer had interest in playing with those things.

Crooked Trees: Building on a Fragile Foundation

Sometimes I do things that I feel like I miss. Sometimes I do not want to be grown and serious and sometimes I do not feel like playing. But whatever I feel, as long as I am not breaking the law, I act on those things. I used to love to take my daughter to Chuck E. Cheese's and play Ski Ball with her. There were times I would take her to the fair knowing I wanted to go as much as her. I build new memories to overshadow the pain of the old ones and this enables me to heal. Even in my writing, I heal. Each time I tell readers about painful experiences, I am shedding dead skin from my life. I no longer cry about things that were painful. I am now able to share my experiences with less tears. I remember crying every time I talked about getting beat up by my abuser. Now, I can share any part of the abuse and not shed a tear. This is what you do with your generational behavior. You war against them. You do not allow them to shame you because now you know that there are other people who have the same obstacles, they just hide it a little better than you. Just as my parents are no longer afraid to tell their truth, I am not afraid to share with my daughter or my husband about my truth.

I am not ashamed to say when I am afraid. I am not afraid to say when I am hurt. I am not afraid to admit when I am wrong, and I am not afraid to speak up when I feel I have been wronged. It does not mean that any of these things are justified, it just allows me to speak up about my shortcomings. There is a world filled with dysfunction. As I write this book, a nine-year-old just hanged herself as a result of being bullied. A two-year-old was killed by a stray bullet. Three people were killed in a local mall, one by the police. Every time I hear these stories, I think that there is a better way for us to resolve these problems. If parents would teach their kids the proper way to love, we will not have bullying. Bullying starts from dysfunction. Innocent bystanders would not lose their lives if those who are carrying the weapons can learn to be less angry. Confrontations would not take place in public places if people would resolve what they are carrying on the inside. We will not have hostile work environments if people would learn how to behave at home and not bring their dysfunctions to work.

Crooked Trees: Building on a Fragile Foundation

Husbands and wives would not disagree if we would just be willing to see the needs of the other person. Everything we see today is the result of unresolved pain.

Unresolved pain is the reason that most of our communities are suffering. It is the reason why 50% of marriages end in divorce and of the 50% that remain, half of them are unhappy. It is the reason for infidelity. It is the reason for gangs, drug use and other negative statistics. Kids are having sex at a younger age in an attempt to find an outlet for the lack of love they are receiving at home. We can argue this matter, but what I speak is what I have lived. Unresolved pain took its toll on me and it is taking its toll on millions of others. The generational behavior that is being passed down from generation to generation is negatively impacting our households and it is spilling over into our communities. There is a great need for everyone to identify with the pain within themselves and work hard to overcome it.

The true test of family was seeing family members criticize the sins of others without acknowledging the sins of themselves.

It Starts with You

I Corinthians 13:10-12 says, *"But when that which is perfect has come, then that which is in part will be done away. When I was a child, I spoke as a child, I thought as a child; but when I became a man, I put away childish things. For now we see in a mirror, darkly, but then face to face."*

This life has not reached its state of perfection. The perfect Kingdom that God has predestined has yet to come. Because of this, what we see around us is less than perfect. But, when Christ returns, that which is perfect will have come. Everything that we allow to matter now, will no longer matter. As children, we do not have a high level of maturity. No matter how intelligent we are, we are still in a childlike state. But once we grow, we should gain such a level of maturity that our childlike demeanor should be set aside. The state we are in now, we only know about the Kingdom of God from what His word says, but there will be a time where we will see His perfect will face to face.

Have you ever heard a new song on the radio? Do you notice that they tend to play it so much that you *get* sick and tired of listening to it? They give one song too much air time. In life, this is what we do with our childhood vices. Years pass and we are still playing the same tune, "Why did this happen to me?" No grievance done against a child should go without justice, but we all have a level of control over our deliverance. **2 Corinthians 5:17 says, *"Therefore if any man be in Christ, he is a new creature: old things are passed away; behold, all things are become new."*** Does this mean what happened in our past no longer exists? No, everything that ever happened is still written in your history, but now your mindset concerning it has changed and so have your reactions. It means that you forgive your offenders and it is not because they deserve it, it's because you care more about your health than holding a grudge. When you can consider the problems of your offender, it helps you to have more compassion so you can forgive. It does not mean that you have to be bosom buddies, it just means that you want to press on pass your past. I love to travel and many times I have heard people say that vacations are expensive. Do you know how many times I have called a travel agent and put a trip on layaway? Do you know how many times I have used booking.com where you can reserve a room now and pay when you get there?

For every vacation I missed as a child, as an adult I put away childish things, and I take vacation. Though I know that is not what the scripture means, I am just showing you that deliverance starts with a better perception. It starts by saying he abused me because he did not know better. It was not his intent to break me, somebody just broke him. When you come to God, it is just your way of saying I want a life better than what I had. Therefore, old memories no longer define me, now I am defined by something new. Your past is what the enemy uses to abort your future. Your biggest battle is not what happened to you, it is what your mind thinks about what happened to you. Our thoughts are our biggest battle, and the best way to overcome what we think is by replacing it with something new. While in therapy, I remember telling my therapist that there were several times when I did not get anything for my birthday or Christmas. She said, "Make a new memory." She told me to ask my husband to buy me a whole lot of gifts, even if some were Dollar Tree gifts and let me sit on the floor and open them up.

I was like a kid at a candy store. He said I was not even looking at what the gifts were, I was just opening them and throwing them to the side. Now, my memories of Christmas are not the times I did not get anything, I now remember the times when I did get something. You have the power to change your circumstances. If you dropped out of school, the only thing that is stopping you from getting a GED is you. Living for God gives you an assurance that things can change. You do not feel let down because daily His word is giving you support, encouragement, and positive affirmations. His word is teaching you to forgive those who offend

Crooked Trees: Building on a Fragile Foundation

you. **Ephesians 4:32 says,** *"And be ye kind to one another, tenderhearted, forgiving one another, even as God for Christ's sake hath forgiven you."* Unforgiveness brings about stress, anger, irritation, and so many other unwarranted symptoms. If you were to go to an ATM and you have never made a deposit, will there be anything available to withdraw? We get out of life what we put into it. If we do not invest in ourselves, we cannot get upset when life yields nothing positive.

I invest 5-6 hours a day listening to a positive resource. Not everyone is able to do this, but I have a desk job and I put on my headphones and listen to things that remind me to be positive. You cannot attract a positive mate if you are negative, nor can you attract positive friends if you are negative. Even if you have not taken drugs a day in your life, learn how to work the twelve steps. Life is about coping skills, the more we learn to cope; the better we are able to handle stress. You cannot force someone who wronged you to admit it, neither can you make them apologize. You can learn to let it go. It will not be a short 24-48-hour process. It did not take you a short time to become bitter and it will not take you a short time to recover. Recovery will take work, but if you put in the work you will yield lifelong benefits. Still, with everything I say, someone still may be in doubt. I will give you an assignment. Purchase a notebook and every morning you need to write down three things in life that you are thankful for. It will be hard at first, but it will get easier as time progresses.

For every bad memory that you have, write out a plan to create a new one. Do not make excuses on this. If you want to try a new restaurant, put money aside little by little and do it. **Psalm 37:4 says,** *"Delight yourself in the Lord, and He will give you the desires of your heart."* Out of everything you do, place your focus on your spiritual well-being. My husband and I were in dire financial strains because his 18-wheeler was in the shop and we had to use all of our money to get it out. Our first anniversary had arrived, and we were going to spend a quiet evening alone at home. One of our friends asked what we were doing, and I told her. She and her husband gave us $150 and made us reservations at a nice restaurant. God is not a gimmick. Since I have connected with God, I can't begin to tell you how many times He has bailed me out. Living for Him is not just limited to the spiritual. It encompasses mind, body, and spirit. God wants us to take care of our full being. Overcoming starts with rebuilding your entire life from scratch. You are no longer bound by what once had control of you. As you recover, do not be afraid of therapy, small groups, or any resource where you can connect to someone who can help you.

Fredrick Douglass has a number of quotes that are meant for rebuilding. My favorite quote of his is, *"It is easier to build strong children than to repair broken men."* It is always easier to catch a child before they are broken, but not always possible. We can, however, do for our children what no one knew to do for us. Mr. Douglass was a firm believer that without struggle, there is no progress. I can tell you that no matter how painful, I am more motivated because of the trials that I have been through. Without my struggles, I could not write this book. I could not minister to other hurt people. I would not have had a desire to go to school for counseling. The struggles of life have a way of pushing you into the area of ministry that God intended for you. We are like the tree that was in front of my Mom's window. After the storm, we appear to be damaged and leaning. When the process of pruning starts, we look worst than we did before the process. We may be crying and bitter because of the storm, but after the pruning, the newness in us begins.

I have never been on drugs, but I learned discipline from studying their process. After being released from a recovery program, they are asked to do 90 meetings in 90 days. How many of you are willing to invest 90 days' worth of positive word in you? This can be through Worship on Sunday, Bible Study, a nightly prayer call (information to be found at the end of this book), or even You-Tube videos. It's about how bad you want to be delivered. I believe I counseled with my Pastor for close to one year. I went to therapy with a professional for about the same period of time. I joined a gym and started to exercise and attended church faithfully. There are times when people reach out to me and ask for my help. I give them one assignment and it is never completed. Normally, those who I give an assignment to that never complete it, tend to be the ones that always relapse back into a funk and have to call me again. When you want to be delivered, there is no such thing as too many resources. Here is just a snippet of the books that I have in my possession:

- *Leaving Yesterday Behind by William Hines*
- *Seeing with New Eyes by David Powlinson*
- *Curing the Heart by Howard Eyrich and William Hines*
- *Boundaries: When to Say Yes, How to Say No to Take Control of Your Life by Henry Cloud and John Townsend*
- *The Five Love Languages by Gary C. Chapman*
- *The Battlefield of the Mind by Joyce Meyer*
- *Me and My Big Mouth by Joyce Meyer*
- *Discontentment: Why Am I So Unhappy? By Lou Priolo*
- *The Complete Husband by Lou Priolo*

How will you know you are serious about being delivered, when you start investing in resources? If you never invest in something as simple as a notebook to write down the three things each morning you are thankful for, you are not ready. If you never listen to a free You-Tube video concerning subject matter that you have issues with, then you are not ready. Signs of readiness start by subtle moves that start you to going in a different direction. I can't sum up my life in one book. I only gave examples in this book. Soon, I will release a biography on my life detailing as much as I possibly can about what God gave me the strength to overcome. Often people write books and encourage you without telling much at all about what they have had to face. I am an open book because I believe through faith, deliverance is possible.

Crooked Trees: Building on a Fragile Foundation

You have the power to change your circumstances.

Crooked Trees: Building on a Fragile Foundation

Let's start this journey together. If you have any prayer requests, you can email me at abbasheartinc@yahoo.com. I have a dedicated team who is on standby to pray diligently over requests. You can join us for prayer Monday through Friday at 7pm CST at 712-770-4700 code 477451. You can even follow us on Facebook at Abba's Heart Inc. Our mission is to encourage God's people to live their best life. Another great resource is the Emmaus Community, if you are in the Birmingham area, please visit bhamemmaus.org. Participating in this retreat and going back to volunteer also changed my life. The Emmaus Community is ecumenical meaning, it welcomes all denomination and respects that we all may worship God in a different way.

If you are a young woman between the age of 15-21 you can find assistance with Woman of Worth. This is a small group that teaches young women about building their self-image. You can reach them at speak2motivateme@gmail.com. This group is not limited to just emotional building, it also teaches you how to be financially literate as well. Of course, I will suggest that your first step be to find a church home. This way, you can find a support system that will assist you in walking in your purpose. Remember change is a process. This means that you will not change overnight. You cannot get frustrated with yourself if you backslide. You must know that victory is in persistence, don't quit even if you have the slightest failure.

With everything starting with you, it is just you learning how to utilize your strengths in order to overcome your weaknesses. It is realizing that, "Adversity is knowing during the midst of the tears that the pain you feel won't last." God sent His Son to make a sacrifice and when we live with regrets, we pull the sacrifice out of love. Therefore, the best way to overcome pain is to know pain isn't pretty until you realize it's filled with purpose. We hear these

Crooked Trees: Building on a Fragile Foundation

things all the time and while we wipe away our tears, we wonder how purpose can be found in pain. Think of working out, in order to build muscle, one has to go through strenuous activity. The purpose for pain in a workout is to get physically fit and build muscle. The purpose in pain when it comes to your life has all to do with what you were born for.

The moment we realize why we were born is the moment that life starts to matter. As long as you are wasting time on attempting to figure out dysfunction, the more you feel sorry for yourself and watch as your life has no fruit. I spent years feeling sorry for myself. I wanted a do-over when it came to my life. I spent so much time wishing the bad away, that I did not recognize the good. It was when I began to work on myself that life started producing all kinds of fruit. I am not saying that I have arrived, there are still some areas where I am weak to the touch. Still, I started. If this reading leaves you with nothing else, I pray that it motivates you to start and continue. We all have a family tree, some are healthier than others. It never matters how you start in life, it only matters how you finish.

Resources

- You-Tube- The Family I Had by Charity Lee
- You-Tube- Crimes That Shook Britain
- Livescience.com-Laura Geggel September 12,2017
- Psychology Today- Sean Grover LCSW November 30,2017
- www.americanaddictioncenters.org
- Power of Positivity- Dr. Mai Stafford

www.powerofpositivity.com

9 Behaviors People Who Grew Up in a Controlling Family Display in Their Adult Lives

- www.woundedsouls.com
- www.learning-mind.com
- www.innerchange.com

Author's Bio

Eboni L. Vasser is founder of Abba's Heart Inc. which is a faith-based non-profit organization that focuses on helping those in the community that struggle with maturing spiritually, mentally, and physically. She is married to Marcus Sr. and together they have three children; Marcus Jr., Antania, and Omar. She is an ordained Evangelist and attends Providence Christian Ministries under the leadership of Apostle and Mrs. Victor L. Hill. She is a volunteer with the Alabama  Justice Ministries and Kairos, which both focus on ministering to individuals who are incarcerated. She is also a member of the Emmaus Community, which focuses on enhancing individuals walk with God. She received her certification in Biblical Lay Counseling and is also seeking her Master of Arts in Biblical Counseling from The Birmingham Theological Seminary. She has worked in the financial fraud industry for the past 19 years and is hoping to transition into full-time ministry. For going on three years, she has led the Abba's Heart Prayer Call which is Monday through Friday at 7pm CST and includes holidays.

Made in the USA
Lexington, KY
19 May 2019